Team Spirit

THE DETROIT TIGERS

BY

MARK STEWART

Content Consultant
James L. Gates, Jr.
Library Director
National Baseball Hall of Fame and Museum

NORWOOD HOUSE PRESS

CHICAGO, ILLINOIS

Norwood House Press
P.O. Box 316598
Chicago, Illinois 60631

For information regarding Norwood House Press, please visit our website at:
www.norwoodhousepress.com or call 866-565-2900.

All photos courtesy of AP Images—AP/Wide World Photos, Inc., except the following:
Author's Collection: (9 bottom, 21 bottom, 33, 34 bottom right);
F.W. Rueckheim & Brother (6 right); Bowman Gum Co. (14);
Goudey Gum Co. (16 left, 29); Gum, Inc. (16 right, 21 top);
Exhibit Supply Co. (20); John Klein (22, 23 top, 36 top, 37 bottom);
Topps, Inc. (26, 35 top left and bottom left and right, 36 bottom, 39 both, 40 both, 43);
Turkey Red (30); Piedmont Tobacco (6 left, 31, 34 bottom left).
Special thanks to Topps, Inc.

Editor: Mike Kennedy
Designer: Ron Jaffe
Project Management: Black Book Partners, LLC.

Special thanks to Jonathan Richards and Dr. Steven Aquino.

Library of Congress Cataloging-in-Publication Data

Stewart, Mark, 1960-
 The Detroit Tigers / by Mark Stewart ; content consultant James L.
Gates, Jr.
   p. cm. -- (Team spirit)
 Summary: "Presents the history, accomplishments and key personalities of
the Detroit Tigers baseball team. Includes timelines, quotes, maps, glossary
and websites"--Provided by publisher.
 Includes bibliographical references and index.
 ISBN-13: 978-1-59953-093-2 (library edition : alk. paper)
 ISBN-10: 1-59953-093-7 (library edition : alk. paper)
 1. Detroit Tigers (Baseball team)--History--Juvenile literature. I. Title.

GV875.D6S79 2007
796.357'640977434--dc22

                                        2006033901

COVER PHOTO: Mike Maroth and Placido Polanco celebrate
a win during the 2006 playoffs.

Table of Contents

SPORTS WORDS & VOCABULARY WORDS: In this book, you will find many words that are new to you. You may also see familiar words used in new ways. The glossary on page 46 gives the meanings of baseball words, as well as "everyday" words that have special baseball meanings. These words appear in **bold type** throughout the book. The glossary on page 47 gives the meanings of vocabulary words that are not related to baseball. They appear in ***bold italic type*** throughout the book.

Meet the Tigers

When baseball fans enter a stadium and take their seats, they want to see their team play a fun, exciting game. The Detroit Tigers feel the same way. They have always put players on the field who make their fans smile. Some of baseball's greatest hitters and pitchers have played for the Tigers, and—win or lose—they almost always give their opponents a tough game.

When a player pulls on the Tigers uniform and wears their famous D on his cap, he becomes a part of baseball history. He knows he is representing a city that has been part of the **American League (A.L.)** for more than 100 years, and must honor the great players who came before him.

This book tells the story of the Tigers. They are a team that likes to swing the bat and score runs, and their fans love to win. No matter what the score of a game, opponents know to never turn their backs on Detroit. At any moment, the Tigers might pounce!

Ivan Rodriguez is congratulated by happy teammates after a big win during the 2006 season.

Way Back When

The Tigers played their first season in 1901 as members of the new American League. In their first game, they were behind 13–4 in the bottom of the ninth inning. The Tigers scored 10 runs to win. For the next century, this was the kind of baseball that Detroit fans came to expect from their team.

The Tigers won the **pennant** each season from 1907 to 1909. This great team was led by Sam Crawford and Ty Cobb, and managed by Hughie Jennings. Crawford was the league's most powerful **slugger**, Cobb was its most feared batter and baserunner, and Jennings was an expert in the strategies of old-time baseball.

COBB, DETROIT

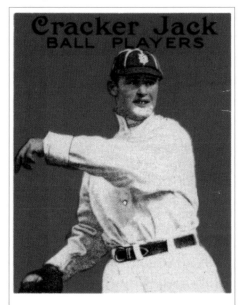

Cracker Jack
BALL PLAYERS

CRAWFORD, DETROIT - AMERICANS

The Tigers were fun to watch in their early years, but they did not win another pennant until the 1930s. This team was led by its catcher, Mickey Cochrane, who was also the manager. His **lineup** starred some of the best hitters in history, including the "G-Men"—Hank Greenberg, Charlie Gehringer, and Goose Goslin. The Tigers captured the pennant in 1934 and 1935, and beat the Chicago Cubs in the '35 **World Series** for their first championship. The Tigers won pennants again in 1940 and 1945. In '45, they won their second championship. This team was led by pitching star Hal Newhouser.

During the 1950s, the Tigers found more young players for their lineup, including pitchers Jim Bunning and Frank Lary, and hitters Harvey Kuenn and Al Kaline. Kaline went straight from high school to the **major leagues** and won a batting championship when he was just 20 years old.

Kaline was still playing for the Tigers when they won their next championship, in 1968. Pitchers Denny McLain and Mickey Lolich led this team, but as always, Detroit had a lot of power in its lineup.

TOP LEFT: Ty Cobb
BOTTOM LEFT: Sam Crawford
ABOVE: Hal Newhouser pitched the Tigers to their second championship, in 1945.

Besides Kaline, the Tigers had sluggers such as Willie Horton, Norm Cash, Jim Northrup, and Bill Freehan—the league's best catcher during the 1960s.

Detroit's greatest team may have been the 1984 Tigers. They were in first place from the first day of the year until the last. This club was led by two young **infielders**, Lou Whitaker and Alan Trammell, heavy hitters Lance Parrish and Kirk Gibson, and **starting pitcher** Jack Morris. **Relief pitcher** Willie Hernandez won the **Cy Young Award** and was named the league's **Most Valuable Player (MVP)**.

Detroit's manager, Sparky Anderson, was a master at moving players in and out of games. While the Tigers had many fine individual players that year, they are best remembered for winning the championship with a total team effort.

LEFT: Al Kaline had more than 3,000 hits in his 22 seasons with the Tigers.
TOP RIGHT: Alan Trammell and Kirk Gibson
BOTTOM RIGHT: As this souvenir button says, 1984 was "The Year of the Tiger."

The Team Today

The Tigers spent many years trying to recapture the spirit of their great 1984 team. To do so, they decided to *retrace* the steps that led them to their last championship. The Tigers put a young team on the field, and let the players "grow up" together under the watchful eyes of patient managers and a handful of **veterans**.

The Tigers *promoted* a group of pitching **prospects** to the major leagues, including Jeremy Bonderman, Mike Maroth, Nate Robertson, Joel Zumaya, and Justin Verlander. They also signed **Gold Glove** catcher Ivan Rodriguez, and veteran pitchers Todd Jones and Kenny Rogers to help with the young staff.

In 2006, the pitchers began to win games they had once lost. As the team gained confidence, hitters such as Brandon Inge, Craig Monroe, Curtis Granderson, and Carlos Guillen started to fulfill their potential. After many seasons of frustration and losing, the Tigers became A.L. champions again.

Justin Verlander warms up with teammates during Spring Training. The Tigers became a winning team when their young pitchers gained confidence.

TIGERS

ComericA
PARK

BOBBY ABREU
OUTS   HR
   5   1
Longest HR tonight 517 FT.

veri on wireless

Labatt Blue

CHEERS.
TO FRIENDS.

Trusted
by the
Pros

henryford.com

SBC

BELLE
TIRE

A better
job
awaits

GOLD BALL
TALLY
$273,000

ROOF
ONE
Residential • Commercial
1-866-ROOF-100

PEPSI

Sports Station 1270

Hit n Hide

11:02 PM 78°F

345'   Rock 800-333-ROCK   BUD LIGHT

Home Turf

For more than 80 years, the team played its home games in Tiger Stadium. The ballpark was called Navin Field when it opened on April 12th, 1912. On the very same day, Fenway Park opened in Boston, Massachusetts. Neither story made the next morning's headlines. Instead, the country's newspapers reported the sinking of the *Titanic*.

The Tigers moved into Comerica Park in 2000. It was a brand-new ballpark, except for home plate, which was brought over from Tiger Stadium. Because there is no upper deck in the outfield, fans have a wonderful view of the Detroit skyline. Under the stands, fans can take a "walk through history" along the stadium's *concourse*. It features a display that traces the story of life and baseball in Detroit since the 1800s.

COMERICA PARK BY THE NUMBERS

- *There are 40,950 seats in the Tigers' ballpark.*
- *The distance from home plate to the left field foul pole is 345 feet.*
- *The distance from home plate to the center field fence is 420 feet.*
- *The distance from home plate to the right field foul pole is 330 feet.*
- *The Tigers' main scoreboard is 180 feet wide.*

The Tigers hosted the 2005 All-Star Game at Comerica Park. The stadium's scoreboard follows Bobby Abreu's progress during the Home Run Derby.

Dressed for Success

The Tigers got their nickname during the 1890s, when they were still a **minor-league** team. They wore socks with yellow and black stripes, which reminded people of this fierce animal. In 1901, the Detroit players wore a cap with a tiger on the front. A few years later, the team started using an Old English-style D on their uniforms and caps.

Over the next 100 years, the Tigers had many different uniform designs. Team colors included orange, black, red, white, and blue. Even when the Detroit uniform had a modern look, the traditional D was still used to keep a connection with the past. In 1995, the Tigers switched to a uniform that reminded fans of the style worn by the championship teams of the 1930s and 1960s.

Johnny Pesky bends for a ground ball in the team's road uniform from the early 1950s.

UNIFORM BASICS

The baseball uniform has not changed much since the Tigers began playing. It has four main parts:

- a cap or batting helmet with a sun visor
- a top with a player's number on the back
- pants that reach down between the ankle and the knee
- stirrup-style socks

The uniform top sometimes has a player's name on the back. The team's name, city, or *logo* is usually on the front. Baseball teams wear light-colored uniforms when they play at home, and darker styles when they play on the road.

For more than 100 years, baseball uniforms were made of wool *flannel* and were very baggy. This helped the sweat *evaporate* and gave players the freedom to move around. Today's uniforms are made of *synthetic* fabrics that stretch with players and keep them dry and cool.

Ivan Rodriguez in Detroit's 2006 white home uniform.

We Won!

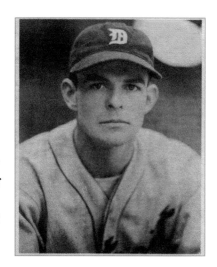

The Tigers won four championships between 1935 and 1984. Each team was led by a group of great stars. The 1935 Tigers won the pennant thanks to veterans Charlie Gehringer, Mickey Cochrane, and Goose Goslin, and the power hitting of young Hank Greenberg. Greenberg's wrist was broken by a pitch in the World Series, but the Detroit players pulled together and beat the Chicago Cubs four games to two. Pitcher Tommy Bridges won twice for the Tigers, and Goslin drove in the winning run in the bottom of the ninth inning of the final game.

Hank Greenberg

Ten years later, the Tigers captured their second championship. Greenberg was now the veteran leader of the Tigers, and pitcher Hal Newhouser was the team's young star. Greenberg hit a **grand slam** on the final day of the 1945 season to win the pennant, and Newhouser led the A.L. in wins, strikeouts, and **earned run average (ERA)**. Both were at their best in the World Series, again against the Cubs. The Tigers won four games to three.

The Tigers won their next pennant in 1968. This team was led by Denny McLain, who won 31 games. As usual, the Tigers had a lineup full of heavy hitters, including Al Kaline, Willie Horton, Bill Freehan, Norm Cash, and Jim Northrup. In all, eight different Tigers hit at least 10 home runs during the season. However, it was the pitching of Mickey Lolich that made the difference in their World Series meeting with the St. Louis Cardinals. Lolich won Game Two, Game Five, and Game Seven to bring a third championship to Detroit.

Like the 1968 team, the 1984 Tigers were led by a group of talented and experienced players. Pitchers Jack Morris, Willie Hernandez, and Aurelio Lopez helped Detroit win 35 of their first 40 games. Lance Parrish was the team's catcher and most powerful

TOP LEFT: Tommy Bridges   **BOTTOM LEFT**: Hank Greenberg
ABOVE: Catcher Bill Freehan blocks home plate and tags out Lou Brock in Game Five of the 1968 World Series. The Tigers won this game and the next two to capture the championship.

hitter, while shortstop Alan Trammell and second baseman Lou Whitaker were baseball's best double-play partners. The heart of the team was its right fielder, Kirk Gibson. He put a charge into the crowd whether the Tigers were at home or on the road, and *inspired* his teammates game after game.

That year, the Tigers defeated the San Diego Padres in the World Series four games to one. Morris won two games, Hernandez **saved** Detroit's two other victories, and Trammell batted .450 for the series. Gibson made several good fielding plays against San Diego, and was the hero in Game Five. With the score tied 3–3 in the fifth inning, he **tagged up** from third base and slid home safely on a pop fly to the second baseman. Three innings later, Gibson launched a home run into the upper deck to finish off the Padres and give the Tigers their fourth championship.

The Tigers nearly won their fifth championship in 2006. The team surprised the experts by making it to the **playoffs** just three seasons after losing a league-record 119 games. Pitching was Detroit's strength. Jeremy Bonderman, Justin Verlander, Nate Robertson, Kenny Rogers, Fernando Rodney, Joel Zumaya, and Todd Jones helped the Tigers build the league's best staff.

Detroit's excellent pitching continued against the New York Yankees and Oakland A's in the playoffs. The Tigers beat them both to win the pennant. Unfortunately, the more experienced St. Louis Cardinals were the better team in the World Series. Detroit lost in five games. It was still a magical season that no Tigers fan will ever forget.

LEFT: Kirk Gibson waves to fans during the parade to celebrate the Tigers' 1984 championship. Gibson was one of Detroit's World Series heroes that year.   **RIGHT**: Magglio Ordonez heads for home after his home run that won the pennant for Detroit in 2006.

Go-To Guys

To be a true star in baseball, you need more than a quick bat and a strong arm. You have to be a "go-to guy"—someone the manager wants on the pitcher's mound or in the batter's box when it matters most. Tigers fans have had a lot to cheer about over the years, including these great stars…

THE PIONEERS

SAM CRAWFORD   Outfielder

- BORN: 4/18/1880 • DIED: 6/15/1968 • PLAYED FOR TEAM: 1903 TO 1917

Sam Crawford hit the baseball farther than anyone else in the early 1900s. In the big ballparks of that time, these hits were often triples instead of home runs. Crawford still holds the record with 309 three-base hits.

HARRY HEILMANN   Outfielder

- BORN: 8/3/1894   • DIED: 7/9/1951
- PLAYED FOR TEAM: 1914 TO 1929

Harry Heilmann was Detroit's best hitter in the 1920s. He won four batting championships between 1921 and 1927.

ABOVE: Harry Heilmann   **TOP RIGHT**: Charlie Gehringer
BOTTOM RIGHT: Al Kaline answers fan mail in front of his locker.

TY COBB · Outfielder

- BORN: 12/18/1886 · DIED: 7/17/1961 · PLAYED FOR TEAM: 1905 TO 1926

Ty Cobb was a fierce and talented player who did whatever it took to win. He was disliked by opponents, but also greatly respected. Cobb won 11 batting championships and retired with a .366 average—the highest in history.

CHARLIE GEHRINGER · Second Baseman

- BORN: 5/11/1903 · DIED: 1/21/1993
- PLAYED FOR TEAM: 1924 TO 1942

Charlie Gehringer was so smooth as a hitter and fielder, and so quiet as a person, that he was nicknamed the "Mechanical Man." He got more than 200 hits in a season seven times and won the batting championship in 1937.

HANK GREENBERG · First Baseman/Outfielder

- BORN: 1/1/1911 · DIED: 9/4/1986
- PLAYED FOR TEAM: 1930, 1933 TO 1941 & 1945 TO 1946

Hank Greenberg was one of the greatest right-handed sluggers in history. Because of injuries and time spent in the Army, he played only eight full seasons for the Tigers. He led the A.L. in home runs and **runs batted in (RBIs)** four times, and won two MVP awards.

AL KALINE · Outfielder

- BORN: 12/19/1934 · PLAYED FOR TEAM: 1953 TO 1974

Al Kaline was often called the "perfect player." He was a very good hitter and a quick and graceful fielder. Kaline finished second in the A.L. MVP voting in 1955 and 1963.

MODERN STARS

ALAN TRAMMELL   Shortstop

- BORN: 2/21/1958
- PLAYED FOR TEAM: 1977 TO 1996

Alan Trammell was the Tigers' greatest shortstop. He won four Gold Gloves and batted .300 seven times. Trammell was the MVP of the 1984 World Series.

JACK MORRIS   Pitcher

- BORN: 5/16/1955
- PLAYED FOR TEAM: 1977 TO 1990

Jack Morris led the Tigers in wins each year from 1979 to 1988. He won more games than anyone in baseball during the 1980s, and pitched two **complete games** in the 1984 World Series.

KIRK GIBSON   Outfielder

- BORN: 5/28/1957
- PLAYED FOR TEAM: 1979 TO 1987 & 1993 TO 1995

Kirk Gibson had amazing power, tremendous speed, and a talent for making great plays when the Tigers needed them most. He led the team in stolen bases four years in a row.

ABOVE: Alan Trammell
TOP RIGHT: Cecil Fielder   **BOTTOM RIGHT**: Justin Verlander

CECIL FIELDER   **First Baseman**

• BORN: 9/21/1963   • PLAYED FOR TEAM: 1990 TO 1996

Cecil Fielder was the star of the Tigers in the early 1990s. He led the A.L. in home runs with 51 in 1990 and 44 in 1991. In 1992, he tied an A.L. record first set by Ty Cobb when he led the league in RBIs for the third year in a row.

JEREMY BONDERMAN   **Pitcher**

• BORN: 10/28/1982

• FIRST YEAR WITH TEAM: 2003

In 2003, 20-year-old Jeremy Bonderman was a member of the Detroit team that lost 119 games. The lessons he learned from that difficult season helped him become one of the team's young leaders.

JUSTIN VERLANDER   **Pitcher**

• BORN: 2/20/1983

• FIRST YEAR WITH TEAM: 2005

The Tigers decided not to rush Justin Verlander to the majors after drafting him in 2004. Instead, *he* rushed the *Tigers*. In 2006, only three pitchers in all of baseball won more games than Verlander.

On the Sidelines

The Tigers have had some of baseball's most famous managers, including Hughie Jennings, Mickey Cochrane, Del Baker, Steve O'Neill, Mayo Smith, and Billy Martin. In 1979, the Tigers hired Sparky Anderson to manage the team. He had led the Cincinnati Reds to four **National League (N.L.)** pennants during the 1970s.

Anderson was the perfect man to teach Detroit's young players. He liked to give everyone a chance to get in the game. Anderson put his players in situations in which they were likely to succeed. He also taught them how to learn from their mistakes. In 1984, his Tigers won the championship.

In 2006, the team hired Jim Leyland as its manager. Like Anderson, he knew how to make players believe in themselves. Leyland had turned losing teams into winners with the Pittsburgh Pirates and Florida Marlins. In his first season in Detroit, the Tigers had the best record in baseball for most of the year, and reached the World Series for the first time since 1984.

Jim Leyland shakes Placido Polanco's hand after a Detroit victory. Leyland led the Tigers to the playoffs in his first season as the team's manager.

One Great Day

When the Tigers and St. Louis Cardinals met in Game Seven of the 1968 World Series, not many people thought Detroit had a chance. The Cardinals handed the ball to Bob Gibson, baseball's best pitcher. He had already beaten the Tigers twice, allowing only one run in 18 innings. In Game One, he set a record by striking out 17 Detroit batters.

MICKEY LOLICH
PITCHER
TIGERS

The only man standing between the Cardinals and the championship was Mickey Lolich of the Tigers—and it was a miracle that he was even standing. As a boy, he was in a motorcycle accident. During his recovery, he noticed that his left arm had become much stronger than his right arm. Even though he was born right-handed, he began pitching left-handed.

Lolich had used his sinking fastball and quick-breaking **slider** to beat the Cardinals in Game Two and Game Five. Detroit's manager, Mayo Smith, asked him to start Game Seven on just two days of rest.

LEFT: Mickey Lolich, who won three games in the 1968 World Series.
RIGHT: The Tigers lift Lolich off the ground after his victory in Game Seven.

Lolich and Gibson battled each other inning after inning. Neither team could move a runner past first base, and both teams made excellent fielding plays. Lou Brock and Curt Flood, the Cardinals' two fastest runners, each made it to first base in the sixth inning, and planned to steal second. Lolich picked them both off before they had the chance.

The Tigers and Cardinals began the seventh inning in a 0–0 tie. With two outs, Norm Cash and Willie Horton hit singles. The next batter, Jim Northrup, hit a line drive to deep center field off Gibson. Flood misjudged the ball for an instant, and could not get back in time to catch it. Two runs scored, and the Tigers went on to win 4–1.

Most baseball fans knew very little about Lolich before the World Series—but that soon changed. His name was in newspaper headlines all over the country. "All of my life, somebody has been the big star and Mickey Lolich was the number-two guy," he said after Game Seven. "I figured my day would come, and this was it."

Legend Has It

Which Detroit pitcher talked to baseballs on the mound?

LEGEND HAS IT that Mark Fidrych did. Fidrych looked more like a Little Leaguer than a major leaguer when he pitched for the Tigers in 1976. The fidgety **rookie** not only talked to the baseball, he jumped for joy after outs, and shook hands with his infielders after good plays. Before each inning, Fidrych would drop to his knees and rearrange the dirt on the mound to his liking. In the locker room, teammates howled with laughter when he did a strange dance called "The Fried Egg." Detroit fans adored Fidrych and nicknamed him "The Bird." Almost a million people came to watch his 29 starts in 1976. Sadly, Fidrych was injured in Spring Training the following year and won just 10 more games.

ABOVE: Mark Fidrych was baseball's most popular pitcher during the 1976 season.
RIGHT: Rudy York, who sizzled all month long in August 1937.

Which Tiger had the best month in team history?

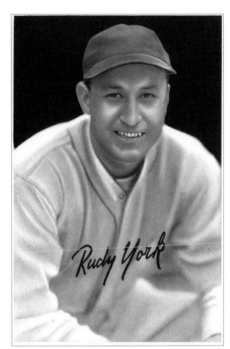

LEGEND HAS IT that Rudy York did. In August of 1937, York smashed 18 home runs and drove in 49 runs for Detroit. Both are still A.L. records. York's unforgettable August is all the more amazing when you realize that he was just a rookie at the time. To add even more pressure, fans and players in other cities tried to distract York by saying mean things about his Native American **heritage**.

Which Tiger once threw a lime over a church?

LEGEND HAS IT that Joel Zumaya did. In the 2006 playoffs, Zumaya's fastball reached 103 miles per hour. But back when he was a teenager, he had no idea how strong his arm was. All he knew was that he loved to throw things. One day Zumaya was standing in front of his house, holding a lime. For no reason in particular, he decided to see how far he could throw it. He heaved the lime down the street, toward the end of his block. It sailed through the air and went completely over the church at the corner!

It Really Happened

COBB DETROIT

T he 1912 Tigers may not have been a great team, yet as long as their star, Ty Cobb, was in the lineup, they always had a chance. During a May game in New York, a rowdy fan insulted Cobb, and Cobb did something an athlete should never do—he went into the stands and fought with the fan. The A.L. *suspended* Cobb without giving him a chance to explain his actions, and did not say when he would be allowed to play again.

Cobb's teammates thought his punishment was unfair. They refused to play until his suspension was lifted. Detroit's manager, Hughie Jennings, had to put a team on the field in Philadelphia the next day, or the club would be fined $5,000 by the league. Jennings made two of his coaches play, and a friend of the manager's found the rest of his team at nearby St. Joseph's College. He offered the players $10 each for the game.

Allan Travers pitched for the Tigers. He later admitted that he had never pitched a full game in his life. Travers did fine for a few innings. He threw the ball so slowly that the Philadelphia

JENNINGS, DETROIT

hitters were not used to it. However, when they discovered that none of the Detroit infielders knew how to field a **bunt**, the bases started to look like a merry-go-round. Travers pitched eight innings, and gave up 26 hits and 24 runs. He walked eight batters and the Tigers made nine errors. The final score was 24–2.

After the game, Cobb thanked his teammates for their support. He told them to get back in uniform—there was no need to embarrass the team again. In the end, the league fined Cobb only $50 and reduced his suspension to just 10 days. The games he missed hardly mattered. Cobb still led the A.L. with 226 hits and a .409 batting average.

LEFT: Ty Cobb was baseball's best hitter, but he also had a terrible temper.
RIGHT: Hughie Jennings managed the Tigers with great energy, but nothing could have helped his team of "replacements."

Team Spirit

The bond between the Tigers and the fans of Detroit goes back more than a century. In 1968, that bond was put to the test. In many American cities, protests against **racial injustice**, poverty, and the Vietnam War exploded into riots. Detroit had already seen some of the same violence and unrest.

The Tigers had a great season, and gave the city the pride it needed to survive the summer of '68. They understood they were playing for something more important than the pennant, and the fans seemed to know this, too. When the Tigers defeated the St. Louis Cardinals in a thrilling World Series, the entire city came together as one.

The Tigers and their fans are still very close. The team's new stadium was a wonderful "thank you" to the people of Detroit, who have worked hard to modernize the city's downtown area. Comerica Park has been a big part of that effort.

LEFT: Detroit fans like to show their "stripes" at Comerica Park.
ABOVE: The fans at Tiger Stadium show their support during the 1960s.

Timeline

Members of the 1935 Tigers pose in the dugout before a World Series game.

1901
The Tigers finish third in their first season.

1935
The Tigers win their first championship.

1945
Hal Newhouser leads the A.L. in wins, strikeouts, and ERA.

1907
Ty Cobb leads the Tigers to their first pennant.

1943
Detroit rookie Dick Wakefield leads the A.L. with 200 hits.

COBB, DETROIT

Ty Cobb batted .350 in 1907.

Dick Wakefield with the 1943 batting champion, Luke Appling.

'74 Highlights

KALINE JOINS 3000 HIT CLUB

Al Kaline

Magglio Ordonez
celebrates Detroit's
return to the playoffs
in 2006.

1974
Al Kaline gets his
3,000th hit.

1992
Cecil Fielder leads the A.L. in
RBIs for the third year in a row.

1968
The Tigers win their
third championship.

1984
The Tigers win their
fourth championship.

2006
The Tigers win the A.L.
pennant for the first time
since 1984.

★ The Sporting News ★

1968 WORLD SERIES SPECIAL

**TIGERS CELEBRATE
THEIR VICTORY**

Detroit's Heroes Go Wild

Detroit's Dick McAuliffe, Denny McLain and Willie Horton spent happy times after winning 1968 World Series.

Dick McAuliffe,
Denny McLain,
and Willie Horton
celebrate in 1968.

Jack Morris, who
won two games
in the 1984
World Series.

TIGERS
PITCHER JACK MORRIS

Fun Facts

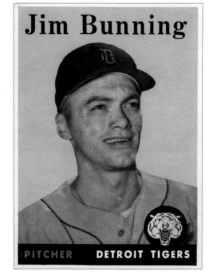

BEST OF BOTH LEAGUES

When the Tigers won the 1984 World Series, Sparky Anderson became the first manager to win championships in the A.L. and N.L. Nine years earlier he managed the Cincinnati Reds to the title.

VOICE OF THE TIGERS

One of baseball's most beloved radio announcers was Ernie Harwell. He called games for the Tigers for more than 40 seasons beginning in 1960.

PITCHING POLITICS

Jim Bunning was Detroit's top pitcher during the 1950s. He led the A.L. in strikeouts twice and pitched a no-hitter in 1958. After leaving baseball, Bunning became a U.S. senator.

TOP LEFT: Sparky Anderson **BOTTOM LEFT**: Jim Bunning
TOP RIGHT: Ty Cobb **BOTTOM RIGHT**: Curtis Pride

WELL AGED

In 1959, a sportswriter asked Ty Cobb how he would do against the pitchers of that time. Cobb thought for a moment and said he would only bat .300. "Of course," he added, "you have to remember, I'm seventy-three!"

HOOP DREAMS

Harry Heilmann was known as a great hitter for the Tigers in the 1920s, but few fans realized that he was also a basketball pioneer. Heilmann owned the Brooklyn Arcadians, one of the best *professional* basketball teams of the 1920s.

A MATTER OF PRIDE

In 1996, the Tigers signed Curtis Pride, a hearing-impaired outfielder. Pride could not hear the sounds of the game, but he could feel the roar of the crowd in his chest after he got a hit. Pride played in 95 games that season and batted .300—the second highest average on the team.

Talking Baseball

"Everybody's dream is to be in the big leagues, but only one in a million gets here."
—*Jeremy Bonderman, on pitching in the majors*

"To hit 100 miles per hour, that's something. I couldn't believe it when I first saw it!"
—*Justin Verlander, on his superfast fastball*

"Ball players do things backward. First we play, *then* we retire and go to work."
—*Charlie Gehringer, on the strange life of a baseball player*

"When I get through managing, I'm going to open up a kindergarten."
—*Billy Martin, on how childish some athletes can be*

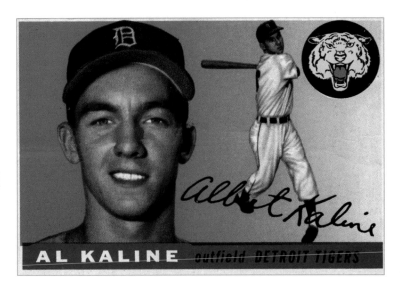

"It looked like a thousand eyes were staring at me saying, 'Who is this young punk?'"

—*Al Kaline, on boarding the Tigers' team bus for the first time at age 18*

"Baseball was one hundred percent of my life."

—*Ty Cobb, on why he played so hard for so long*

"This game is beautiful. I don't think there's anything in the world that can produce so many emotional highs and lows, day in and day out."

—*Bill Freehan, on the magic of baseball*

LEFT: Jeremy Bonderman
TOP RIGHT: Al Kaline
BOTTOM RIGHT: Bill Freehan

For the Record

The great Tigers teams and players have left their marks on the record books. These are the "best of the best"…

Harvey Kuenn

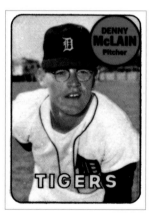

Denny McLain

TIGERS AWARD WINNERS

WINNER	AWARD	YEAR
Mickey Cochrane	Most Valuable Player	1934
Hank Greenberg	Most Valuable Player	1935
Charlie Gehringer	Most Valuable Player	1937
Hank Greenberg	Most Valuable Player	1940
Hal Newhouser	Most Valuable Player	1944
Hal Newhouser	Most Valuable Player	1945
Harvey Kuenn	Rookie of the Year*	1953
Denny McLain	Cy Young Award	1968
Denny McLain	Most Valuable Player	1968
Mickey Lolich	World Series MVP	1968
Denny McLain	Cy Young Award	1969
Mark Fidrych	Rookie of the Year	1976
Lou Whitaker	Rookie of the Year	1978
Sparky Anderson	Manager of the Year	1984
Willie Hernandez	Cy Young Award	1984
Willie Hernandez	Most Valuable Player	1984
Alan Trammell	World Series MVP	1984
Sparky Anderson	Manager of the Year	1987

The Rookie of the Year award is given to the league's best first-year player.

TIGERS ACHIEVEMENTS

ACHIEVEMENT	YEAR
A.L. Pennant Winner	1907
A.L. Pennant Winner	1908
A.L. Pennant Winner	1909
A.L. Pennant Winner	1934
A.L. Pennant Winner	1935
World Series Champions	1935
A.L. Pennant Winner	1940
A.L. Pennant Winner	1945
World Series Champions	1945
A.L. Pennant Winner	1968
World Series Champions	1968
A.L. East Champions	1972
A.L. East Champions	1984
A.L. Pennant Winner	1984
World Series Champions	1984
A.L. East Champions	1987
A.L. Pennant Winner	2006

ABOVE: Willie Hernandez and catcher Lance Parrish lead the celebration after the last out of the 1984 World Series.
LEFT: Magglio Ordonez watches Ivan Rodriguez "low-five" Sean Casey after a home run.

41

Pinpoints

The history of a baseball team is made up of many smaller stories. These stories take place all over the map—not just in the city a team calls "home." Match the push-pins on these maps to the Team Facts and you will begin to see the story of the Tigers unfold!

TEAM FACTS

1 Detroit, Michigan—*The team has played here since 1901.*

2 St. Paul, Minnesota—*Jack Morris was born here.*

3 New York, New York—*Hank Greenberg was born here.*

4 Narrows, Georgia—*Ty Cobb was born here.*

5 Baltimore, Maryland—*Al Kaline was born here.*

6 Bridgewater, South Dakota—*Sparky Anderson was born here.*

7 Wahoo, Nebraska—*Sam Crawford was born here.*

8 Portland, Oregon—*Mickey Lolich was born here.*

9 San Francisco, California—*Harry Heilmann was born here.*

10 Tecamachalco, Mexico—*Aurelio Lopez was born here.*

11 Santo Domingo, Dominican Republic—*Placido Polanco was born here.*

12 Aguada, Puerto Rico—*Willie Hernandez was born here.*

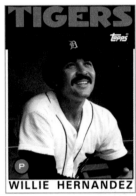

Willie Hernandez

Play Ball

Baseball is a game played between two teams over nine innings. Teams take one turn at bat and one turn in the field during each inning. A turn at bat ends when three outs are made. The batters on the hitting team try to reach base safely. The players on the fielding team try to prevent this from happening.

In baseball, the ball is controlled by the pitcher. The pitcher must throw the ball to the batter, who decides whether or not to swing at each pitch. If a batter swings and misses, it is a strike. If the batter lets a good pitch go by, it is also a strike. If the batter swings and the ball does not stay in fair territory (between the v-shaped lines that begin at home plate) it is called "foul," and is counted as a strike. If the pitcher throws three strikes, the batter is out. If the pitcher throws four bad pitches before that, the batter is awarded first base. This is called a base-on-balls, or "walk."

When the batter swings the bat and hits the ball, everyone springs into action. If a fielder catches a batted ball before it hits the ground, the batter is out. If a fielder scoops the ball off the ground and throws it to first base before the batter arrives, the batter is out. If the batter reaches first base safely, he is credited with a hit. A one-base hit is called a single, a two-base hit is called a double, a three-base hit is called a triple, and a four-base hit is called a home run.

Runners who reach base are only safe when they are touching one of the bases. If they are caught between the bases, the fielders can tag them with the ball and record an out.

A batter who is able to circle the bases and make it back to home plate before three outs are made is credited with a run scored. The team with the most runs after nine innings is the winner.

Anyone who has played baseball (or softball) knows that it can be a complicated game. Every player on the field has a job to do. Different players have different strengths and weaknesses. The pitchers, batters, and managers make hundreds of decisions every game. The more you play and watch baseball, the more "little things" you are likely to notice. The next time you are at a game, look for these plays:

PLAY LIST

DOUBLE PLAY—A play where the fielding team is able to make two outs on one batted ball. This usually happens when a runner is on first base, and the batter hits a ground ball to one of the infielders. The base runner is forced out at second base and the ball is then thrown to first base before the batter arrives.

HIT AND RUN—A play where the runner on first base sprints to second base while the pitcher is throwing the ball to the batter. When the second baseman or shortstop moves toward the base to wait for the catcher's throw, the batter tries to hit the ball to the place that the fielder has just left. If the batter swings and misses, the fielding team can tag the runner out.

INTENTIONAL WALK—A play when the pitcher throws four bad pitches on purpose, allowing the batter to walk to first base. This happens when the pitcher would much rather face the next batter—and is willing to risk putting a runner on base.

SACRIFICE BUNT—A play where the batter makes an out on purpose so that a teammate can move to the next base. On a bunt, the batter tries to "deaden" the pitch with the bat instead of swinging at it.

SHOESTRING CATCH—A play where an outfielder catches a short hit an inch or two above the ground, near the tops of his shoes. It is not easy to run as fast as you can and lower your glove without slowing down. It can be risky, too. If a fielder misses a shoestring catch, the ball might roll all the way to the fence.

Glossary

AMERICAN LEAGUE (A.L.)—One of baseball's two major leagues. The A.L. started play in 1901. The National League began play in 1876.

BUNT—A short hit made by "blocking" a pitch with the bat. A bunt is often used to advance runners who are already on base.

COMPLETE GAMES—Games that the same pitcher starts and finishes.

CY YOUNG AWARD—The trophy given to each league's best pitcher each year.

EARNED RUN AVERAGE (ERA)—A statistic that measures how many runs a pitcher gives up for every nine innings he pitches.

GOLD GLOVE—An award given each year to baseball's best fielders.

GRAND SLAM—A home run with the bases loaded.

INFIELDERS—Defensive players who stand near the bases, including the first baseman, second baseman, third baseman, and shortstop.

LINEUP—The list of players who are playing in a game.

MAJOR LEAGUES—The top level of professional baseball leagues. The A.L. and N.L. make up today's major leagues. Sometimes called the "big leagues" or "majors."

MINOR-LEAGUE—Belonging to one of the professional leagues that are below the major-league level.

MOST VALUABLE PLAYER (MVP)—An award given each year to each league's top player; an MVP is also selected for the World Series and All-Star Game.

NATIONAL LEAGUE (N.L.)—The older of the two major leagues. The N.L. started play in 1876.

PENNANT—A league championship. The term comes from the triangular flag awarded to each season's champion, beginning in the 1870s.

PLAYOFFS—The games played after the regular season to determine which teams will advance to the World Series.

PROSPECTS—Young players who are expected to become stars.

RELIEF PITCHER—A pitcher who is brought into a game to replace another pitcher. Relief pitchers can be seen warming up in the bullpen.

ROOKIE—A player in his first season.

RUNS BATTED IN (RBIs)—A statistic that measures the number of runners a batter drives home.

SAVED—Recorded the last out in a team's win. A pitcher on the mound for the last out of a close victory is credited with a "save."

SLIDER—A fast pitch that curves and drops just as it reaches the batter.

SLUGGER—A powerful hitter.

STARTING PITCHER—The pitcher who begins the game for his team.

TAGGED UP—Ran after a batted ball has been caught.

VETERANS—Players who have great experience.

WORLD SERIES—The world championship series played between the winners of the American and National Leagues.

OTHER WORDS TO KNOW

CONCOURSE—A long passageway.

EVAPORATE—Disappear, or turn into vapor.

FLANNEL—A soft wool or cotton material.

HERITAGE—Ethnic background.

INSPIRED—Encouraged others to action.

LOGO—A symbol or design that represents a company or team.

PROFESSIONAL—Doing a job for money.

PROMOTED—Moved up to a higher level.

RACIAL INJUSTICE—The violation of a person's rights because of their race or ethnic background.

RETRACE—Follow the same line again.

SUSPENDED—Punished by excluding.

SYNTHETIC—Made in a laboratory, not in nature.

Places to Go

ON THE ROAD

DETROIT TIGERS
Comerica Park
2100 Woodward Avenue
Detroit, Michigan 48201-3474
(313) 471-2255

NATIONAL BASEBALL HALL OF FAME AND MUSEUM
25 Main Street
Cooperstown, New York 13326
(888) 425-5633
www.baseballhalloffame.org

ON THE WEB

THE DETRIOT TIGERS
  • *to learn more about the Tigers*

www.Tigers.com

MAJOR LEAGUE BASEBALL
  • *to learn about all the major league teams*

www.mlb.com

MINOR LEAGUE BASEBALL
  • *to learn more about the minor leagues*

www.minorleaguebaseball.com

ON THE BOOKSHELVES

To learn more about the sport of baseball, look for these books at your library or bookstore:

  • Kelly, James. *Baseball*. New York, NY: DK, 2005.

  • Jacobs, Greg. *The Everything Kids' Baseball Book*. Cincinnati, OH: Adams Media Corporation, 2006.

  • Stewart, Mark and Kennedy, Mike. *Long Ball: The Legend and Lore of the Home Run*. Minneapolis, MN: Millbrook Press, 2006.

Index

The Team

MARK STEWART has written more than 25 books on baseball, and over 100 sports books for kids. He grew up in New York City during the 1960s rooting for the Yankees and Mets, and now takes his two daughters, Mariah and Rachel, to the same ballparks. Mark comes from a family of writers. His grandfather was Sunday Editor of the *New York Times* and his mother was Articles Editor of *Ladies' Home Journal* and *McCall's*. Mark has profiled hundreds of athletes over the last 20 years. He has also written several books about his native New York and New Jersey, his home today. Mark is a graduate of Duke University, with a degree in history. He lives with his daughters and wife, Sarah, overlooking Sandy Hook, NJ.

JAMES L. GATES, JR. has served as Library Director at the National Baseball Hall of Fame since 1995. He had previously served in academic libraries for almost fifteen years. He holds degrees from Belmont Abbey College, the University of Notre Dame, and Indiana University. During his career Jim has authored several academic articles and has served in an editorial capacity on multiple book, magazine, and museum publications, and he also serves as host for the Annual Cooperstown Symposium on Baseball and American Culture. He is an ardent Baltimore Orioles fan and enjoys watching baseball with his wife and two children.